# Footfalls

# SAMUEL BECKETT

# FOOTFALLS

FABER AND FABER
London and Boston

*First published in 1976*
*by Faber and Faber Limited*
*3 Queen Square London WC1*
*Reprinted 1978*
*Printed in Great Britain by*
*Latimer Trend & Company Ltd Plymouth*
*All rights reserved*

*ISBN 0 571 11040 1*

All applications for performing rights
in *Footfalls* should be addressed to
Spokesmen, 1 Craven Hill, London W2

*Footfalls* was first performed at
the Royal Court Theatre in the spring
of 1976 during a season mounted to mark
the author's seventieth birthday.

*May (M), dishevelled grey hair, worn grey wrap hiding feet, trailing.*
*Woman's voice (V) from dark upstage.*
*Strip: downstage, parallel with front, length seven steps, width one metre, a little off centre audience right.*

$$\text{L} \frac{\quad r \quad l \quad r \quad l \quad r \quad l \quad r \quad}{\quad l \quad r \quad l \quad r \quad l \quad r \quad l \quad} \text{R}$$

*Pacing: starting with right foot (r) from right (R) to left (L), with left foot (l) from L to R.*
*Turn: rightabout at L, leftabout at R.*
*Steps: clearly audible rhythmic pad.*
*Lighting: dim, strongest at floor level, less on body, least on head.*
*Voices: both low throughout.*

*Curtain. Stage in darkness.*
*Faint single chime. Pause as echoes die.*
*Fade up to dim on strip. Rest in darkness.*
*M discovered pacing approaching L. Turns at L, paces three more lengths, halts facing front at R.*
*Pause.*

M: Mother. (*Pause. No louder.*) Mother.
    (*Pause.*)
V: Yes, May.
M: Were you asleep?
V: Deep asleep. (*Pause.*) I heard you in my deep sleep. (*Pause.*)
    There is no sleep so deep I would not hear you there.
    (*Pause. M resumes pacing. Four lengths. After first length, synchronous with steps.*) One two three four five six seven
    wheel one two three four five six seven wheel. (*Free.*) Will
    you not try to snatch a little sleep?

(M *halts facing front at R. Pause.*)

M: Would you like me to inject you again?

V: Yes, but it is too soon.
   (*Pause.*)

M: Would you like me to change your position?

V: Yes, but it is too soon.
   (*Pause.*)

M: Straighten your pillows? (*Pause.*) Change your drawsheet?
   (*Pause.*) Pass you the bedpan? (*Pause.*) The warming-pan?
   (*Pause.*) Dress your sores? (*Pause.*) Sponge you down?
   (*Pause.*) Moisten your poor lips? (*Pause.*) Pray with you?
   (*Pause.*) For you?
   (*Pause.*)

V: Yes, but it is too soon.
   (*Pause.*)

M: What age am I now?

V: And I? (*Pause. No louder.*) And I?

M: Ninety.

V: So much?

M: Eighty-nine, ninety.

V: I had you late. (*Pause.*) In life. (*Pause.*) Forgive me again.
   (*Pause. No louder.*) Forgive me again.
   (*Pause.*)

M: Well?

V: In your forties.

M: So little?

V: I'm afraid so. (*Pause. M resumes pacing. After first turn at
   L.*) May. (*Pause. No louder.*) May.

M: (*Pacing.*) Yes, Mother.

V: Will you never have done? (*Pause.*) Will you never have done
   . . . revolving it all?

M: (*Pacing.*) It?

V: It all. (*Pause.*) In your poor mind. (*Pause.*) It all. (*Pause.*)
   It all.
   (M *continues pacing. Five seconds. Fade out on strip.*)
   (*All in darkness. Steps silent.*)
   (*Long pause.*)
   (*Chime a little fainter. Pause for echoes.*)

*(Fade up to a little less on strip. Rest in darkness.)*
*(M discovered facing front at R.)*
*(Pause.)*

V: I walk here now. *(Pause.)* Rather I come and stand. *(Pause.)* At nightfall. *(Pause.)* My voice is in her mind. *(Pause.)* She fancies she is alone. *(Pause.)* See how still she stands, how stark, with her face to the wall. *(Pause.)* How outwardly unmoved. *(Pause.)* She has not been out since girlhood. *(Pause.)* She hears in her poor mind, She has not been out since girlhood. *(Pause.)* Not out since girlhood. *(Pause.)* Where is she, it may be asked. *(Pause.)* In the old home, the same where she—— *(Pause.)* The same where she began. *(Pause.)* Where it began. *(Pause.)* It all began. *(Pause.)* But this, this, when did this begin? *(Pause.)* When other girls of her age were out at . . . lacrosse she was already here. *(Pause.)* At this. *(Pause.)* The floor here, now bare, once was—— (M *begins pacing. Steps a little slower.)* But let us watch her move, in silence. (M *paces. Towards end of second length.)* Watch how feat she wheels. (M *turns, paces. Synchronous with steps third length.)* Three four five. (M *turns at L, paces one more length, halts facing front at R.)* I say the floor here, now bare, this strip of floor, once was carpeted, a deep pile. Till one night, while still little more than a child, she called her mother and said, Mother, this is not enough. The mother: Not enough? May—the child's given name—May: Not enough. The mother: What do you mean, May, not enough, what can you possibly mean, May, not enough? May: I mean, Mother, that I must hear the feet, however faint they fall. The mother: The motion alone is not enough? May: No, Mother, the motion alone is not enough, I must hear the feet, however faint they fall. *(Pause.* M *resumes pacing. With pacing.)* Does she still sleep, it may be asked? Yes, some nights she does, in snatches, bows her poor head against the wall and snatches a little sleep. *(Pause.)* Still speak? Yes, some nights she does, when she fancies none can hear. *(Pause.)* Tells how it was. *(Pause.)* Tries to tell how it was. *(Pause.)* It all. *(Pause.)* It all. (M *continues pacing. Five seconds. Fade out on strip.)*
*(All in darkness. Steps silent.)*

*(Long pause.)*
*(Chime a little fainter still. Pause for echoes.)*
*(Fade up to a little less still on strip. Rest in darkness.)*
*(M discovered facing front at R.)*
*(Pause.)*

M: Sequel. A little later, when she was quite forgotten, she
began to—— *(Pause.)* A little later, when as though she
had never been, it never been, she began to walk. *(Pause.)*
At nightfall. *(Pause.)* Slip out at nightfall and into the little
church by the south door, always locked at that hour, and
walk, up and down, up and down, his poor arm. *(Pause.)*
Some nights she would halt, as one frozen by some shudder of
the mind, and stand stark still till she could move again.
But many also were the nights when she paced without pause,
up and down, up and down, before vanishing the way she
came. *(Pause.)* No sound. *(Pause.)* None at least to be heard.
*(Pause.)* The semblance. *(Pause. Begins pacing. Steps a little
slower still. After two lengths halts facing front at R. Pause.)*
Faint, though by no means invisible, in a certain light. *(Pause.)*
Given the right light. *(Pause.)* Grey rather than white, a pale
shade of grey. *(Pause.)* Tattered. *(Pause.)* A tangle of tatters.
*(Pause.)* A faint tangle of pale grey tatters. *(Pause.)* Watch it
pass—*(pause)*—watch her pass before the candelabrum, how
its flames, their light . . . like moon through passing rack.
*(Pause.)* Soon then after she was gone, as though never there,
began to walk, up and down, up and down, that poor arm.
*(Pause.)* At nightfall. *(Pause.)* That is to say, at certain seasons
of the year, during Vespers. *(Pause.)* Necessarily. *(Pause.
Begins pacing. After one length halts facing front at L. Pause.)*
Old Mrs Winter, whom the reader will remember, old Mrs
Winter, one late autumn Sunday evening, on sitting down to
supper with her daughter after worship, after a few half-
hearted mouthfuls laid down her knife and fork and bowed her
head. What is it, Mother, said the daughter, a most strange
girl, though scarcely a girl any more . . . *(brokenly)* . . .
dreadfully—— *(Pause. Normal voice.)* What is it, Mother, are
you not feeling yourself? *(Pause.)* Mrs W. did not at once
reply. But finally, raising her head and fixing Amy—the

daughter's given name, as the reader will remember—fixing Amy full in the eye she said—(*pause*)—she murmured, fixing Amy full in the eye she murmured, Amy, did you observe anything . . . strange at Evensong? Amy: No, Mother, I did not. Mrs W: Perhaps it was just my fancy. Amy: Just what exactly, Mother, did you perhaps fancy it was? (*Pause.*) Just what exactly, Mother, did you perhaps fancy this . . . strange thing was you observed? (*Pause.*) Mrs W: You yourself observed nothing . . . strange? Amy: No, Mother, I myself did not, to put it mildly. Mrs W: What do you mean, Amy, to put it mildly, what can you possibly mean, Amy, to put it mildly? Amy: I mean, Mother, that to say I observed nothing . . . strange is indeed to put it mildly. For I observed nothing of any kind, strange or otherwise. I saw nothing, heard nothing, of any kind. I was not there. Mrs W: Not there? Amy: Not there. Mrs W: But I heard you respond. (*Pause.*) I heard you say Amen. (*Pause.*) How could you have responded if you were not there? (*Pause.*) How could you possibly have said Amen if, as you claim, you were not there? (*Pause.*) The love of God, and the fellowship of the Holy Ghost, be with us all, evermore. Amen. (*Pause.*) I heard you distinctly. (*Pause. Begins pacing. After three steps halts without facing front. Long pause. Resumes pacing, halts facing front at R. Long pause.*) Amy. (*Pause. No louder.*) Amy. (*Pause.*) Yes, Mother. (*Pause.*) Will you never have done? (*Pause.*) Will you never have done . . . revolving it all? (*Pause.*) It? (*Pause.*) It all. (*Pause.*) In your poor mind. (*Pause.*) It all. (*Pause.*) It all.
(*Pause. Fade out on strip. All in darkness.*)
(*Pause.*)
(*Chime even a little fainter still. Pause for echoes.*)
(*Fade up to even a little less still on strip.*)
(*No trace of May.*)
(*Hold fifteen seconds.*)
(*Fade out.*)
(*Curtain.*)